First Facts®

ALL ABOUT MEDIA

WHAT IS MEDIA?

by BRIEN J. JENNINGS

CAPSTONE PRESS
a capstone imprint

First Facts Books are published by Capstone Press,
1710 Roe Crest Drive, North Mankato, Minnesota 56003
www.mycapstone.com

Library of Congress Cataloging-in-Publication Data is available on the Library of Congress website.
ISBN 978-1-5435-0221-3 (library binding)
ISBN 978-1-5435-0225-1 (paperback)
ISBN 978-1-5435-0229-9 (ebook pdf)

Editorial Credits:
Erika L. Shores, editor; Juliette Peters, designer;
Morgan Walters, media researcher; Kathy McColley, production specialist

Photo Credits:
Capstone Studio: Karon Dubke, 5; Shutterstock: advent, 20, Andrey_Popov, 19, Artur. B, design element, Chaiwut, 9, Everett Collection, 14, Iakov Filimonov, 11, lenisecalleja.photography, 15, Maxx-Studio, 17, MNStudio, Cover, mongione, 4, patat, 13, Supphachai Salaeman, design element throughout, TonyV3112, 8, Twin Design, 21, vectorfusionart, 7

Printed and bound in the USA.
010880S18

Table of Contents

Media, Media Everywhere!

Media is talked about all the time because it's everywhere. Look around and you'll see examples all over. Media might be something we hear, see, or even wear on our clothes. Books, TV shows, news reports, the Internet, and video games are also types of media.

Look!

Look at your clothes. Do you see a **logo** anywhere? Logos are an example of media.

What Is Media Literacy?

Media literacy means understanding books, TV shows, stories, music, and their messages. We understand who made the media and why. People write messages for an **audience**. The audience is anyone who might see the media.

logo—a symbol of a company's brand
audience—people who hear, read, or see a message

Getting to Know Media

The word media can mean a lot of things. Media refers to the tools we use to share messages, ideas, and information with other people. There are many types of media. The main types are print, **recorded**, and **broadcast**.

We use media in different ways. Sometimes we listen, watch, or read. Sometimes we do all three at the same time, such as watching a soccer game on TV.

Media is used for three main reasons:
1. To inform or educate
2. To entertain
3. To persuade, which means to make you believe something is true

---

recorded—written so that it can be used or seen again in the future

broadcast—a TV or radio program

Print Media

Print is the oldest type of media. Words or pictures are written on paper, cloth, or another surface. Print media includes newspapers, magazines, and books. **Billboards**, posters, and even your T-shirt with a logo are print media too.

billboard—a large outdoor sign used to advertise products or services

Recordings: Sound and Films

Recordings are sounds or images that are stored. The recordings can be listened to and watched at a later time. When you listen to music or watch a movie, it is most likely a recording.

The first sound recordings were made in the 1800s. They were made using paper, tin foil, or wax. The only way to listen to recordings was to use a phonograph. This machine had to be cranked by hand, and the sound **quality** wasn't very good.

quality—the standard of something as measured against other things of a similar kind

The first film was made in 1878. Today it wouldn't seem like much of a movie at all. It didn't tell a story or have people in it. It was just a horse running. Early films were also silent. The first film with sound came out in 1927.

Over time people came up with new ways to record sound and pictures. People today can listen to music and watch movies almost anywhere using cell phones, laptops, and tablets.

Think About It!

How do you listen to music? Where are some of the places you watch movies or videos?

Broadcast Media

Do you enjoy listening to the radio or watching TV? If so, then you are using broadcast media. This type of media uses radio waves to carry sound and images.

The radio became popular in the 1920s. Most people listened to the radio for news and entertainment until TV took over in the 1950s. TV quickly became a popular source for news and information.

Advertising and the Media

Advertisements are common in a lot of types of media. Advertisements on radio and TV try to get people to buy products and services. Large billboards show photos of famous people or logos. Posters show the newest movies coming to theaters. Can you think of other ways ads are used in different types of media?

---

advertisement—a notice that calls attention to a product or an event

New Media

Computers are all around us. Since the 1990s, computers and digital media have become the most popular ways for people to get their news and entertainment.

People today can read books, magazines, and newspapers using their cell phones and the Internet. TVs also are digital. People can listen to music, stream movies, and play video games on their TVs. People even create their own media using digital media. Online blogs, photo books, and stop-motion films are examples of digital media.

FACT! There are more mobile phones in the world today than people.

Making Media

Media tells or shows a message using words, pictures, and sound. We read, listen to, and watch media everywhere we go. We also write and draw media to share messages and ideas. With a computer, tablet, or smartphone, anyone can create media. Today there are **apps** people use to make videos and record music.

---

app—a program that is downloaded to computers and mobile devices; app is short for application

Try It!

Get ready to make your own media! Tell a story by making your own movie or comic strip. First, think of a short story. Draw three pictures to tell the beginning, middle, and end.

If you can, use a tablet or cell phone to take photos of the three pictures. Ask an adult to help you find an app for filmmaking. Next, follow the instructions to add sound or your voice to the pictures. Then, share your movie or comic strip with your friends and family.

Think About It!

How many examples of media can you find right now? What kinds of media do you see?

Glossary

advertisement (ad-vuhr-TYZ-muhnt)—a notice that calls attention to a product or an event

app (APP)—a program that is downloaded to computers and mobile devices; app is short for application

audience (AW-dee-uhns)—people who hear, read, or see a message

billboard (BIL-bord)—a large outdoor sign used to advertise products or services

broadcast (BRAWD-kast)—a TV or radio program

logo (LOH-goh)—a symbol of a company's brand

quality (KWAHL-uh-tee)—the standard of something as measured against other things of a similar kind

recorded (ri-KOR-dud)—written so that it can be used or seen again in the future

Read More

Bodden, Valerie. *Identify and Evaluate Advertising.* Info Wise. Minneapolis: Lerner Publications Company, 2015.

Gosman, Gillian. *Express It: Sharing Your Media Online.* Core Skills. New York: PowerKids Press, 2015.

Hubbard, Ben. *Using Digital Technology.* Our Digital Planet. Chicago: Heinemann Library, 2017.

Internet Sites

Use FactHound to find Internet sites related to this book:

Visit *www.facthound.com*

Just type in 9781543502213 and go.

 Check out projects, games and lots more at **www.capstonekids.com**

Critical Thinking Questions

1. Describe three types of media.

2. What are the three main reasons we use media?

3. What is the purpose of advertising?

Index